Internet Addiction

When addiction is consumed through the Internet

By
Juan Moisés de la Serna

Translated by Garcia Menendez Maria Gloria

www.juanmoisesdelaserna.es

Preamble

Technology is more and more present in our lives, which is a clear advance, but also a danger, especially among the youngest people, since they can fall into what is called Internet Addiction.

This has become a reality today, a health problem that did not exist only a decade ago, and which is taking on new victims and more and more young people every day.

Although the long-term consequences are still unknown, the fact that some studies indicate that 30% of young people who use the Internet on a daily basis are at risk of developing a behavioural addiction means that one in three of them is at risk of developing a behavioural addiction.

While some countries are beginning to take steps to prevent it, in others they have not yet realized the gravity of the situation, hence the need to disseminate the results of the latest research in this area to give visibility to a social problem that requires both preventive and curative measures.

Index

Dedicated to my parents

THANKS

I would like to take this opportunity to thank all the people who have contributed to this text, especially Mr. Cam Adair, co-author of the Manual on Addiction of Video Games for Parents.

"Internet Addiction: When addiction is consumed through the Internet"

Written By Juan Moises de la Serna

Copyright © 2018 Juan Moises de la Serna

Distributed by TeakTime.

https://www.traduzionelibri.it

Translated by Garcia Menendez Maria Gloria

Chapter 1. Definition of Internet Addiction

The extensive and intensive use of new technologies, especially among young people, has brought about a new reality, that of Internet addiction.

Although this phenomenon has been reported for some years now, Internet addiction has become a "common" mental health problem.

Addictions, especially behavioural ones, do not seem to distinguish between gender or age, and can occur at any time in life, although it is during adolescence that some of them seem to become more evident.

Perhaps because there is a certain level of social permissiveness in young people to explore new behaviours, including risky ones, which are not allowed at any other age.

Some defend this position by indicating that it is a way of discovering the world, but above all oneself, with its possibilities and limitations.

Just like experiencing healthy behaviours, it is also when the first addictive practices appear, either substance or behavioural, such as Internet addiction.

But if there is a particularly sensitive group among young people who are particularly sensitive to Internet addiction, it is university students, on whom a great deal of research is being carried out, although it is not clear whether it is because Internet Addiction has a greater impact on them, or because it is a particularly accessible group for research, in what some have called campus research, but what health problems does the Internet entail?

This is precisely what is being investigated through research conducted jointly by the Department of Community Medicine, HiTech School of Medicine and the Department of Statistics, Utkal University (India), the results of which have been published in the International Journal of Advanced Multidisciplinary Research.

The study included 100 randomly selected students between the ages of 17 and 23, 95% of whom were women.

All of them were given a test to assess their level of Internet addiction through the I.A.T. (Internet Addiction Test) and another to evaluate the implications in the student's emotional world through the P.A.N.A.S. (Positive and Negative Affect Schedule).

Data was also collected on the time they spend on the Internet, the purpose of their use, the places they visit and the number of hours they spend surfing the Internet.

The results show that 74% of Internet use is for personal purposes, while only 26% is for subjects related to their studies.

With 76% of students aged between 2 and 4 years as users of the network, 93% showing non-intensive use of the networks, less than two hours a day.

With respect to the places they visit, 23% do so on

social networks, while the remaining 76% use it to explore the Internet in search of information related to their studies.

Although this is a broad sample, it focuses exclusively on one type of technology career, so the results cannot be extended to other students in less technology-related careers.

Likewise, and despite reporting that both men and women were included in the groups of participants, the data are not analyzed separately, so with this study it is not possible to know the incidence of Internet addiction in relation to gender.

Despite having been evaluated, the results do not indicate the degree of students who are addicted to the Internet, nor do they explain the significant positive effects on mood that have been found in the use of the Internet.

But if one thing should be noted is that the young people in the study spend too much time on "personal issues" that are almost exclusively focused on social networks, compared to those they use for their studies, where the use of the Internet is more widespread.

This should also serve to reflect on the educational model, which is "distant" from the way in which young people interact in the network, and should be incorporated new strategies to "exploit" the possibilities of social networks.

Nowadays it is difficult to think that a young does not has knowledge or an account in Facebook, Twitter or Tuenti among others, because they were born in the era of social networks, considering themselves to be "digital natives", that is, those who were born after the eighties and who had little access to new technologies.

Those who are older, those who were born before the 80s, have to make an effort to keep themselves informed and trained about social networks, and this is what is called "digital immigrants", that is, people who were born without these possibilities and who now have to enter this world, sometimes confused and others disconcerting, but in any case useful and necessary.

As previously it was requested for some jobs to have a driver's license and a minimum level of education, it is now necessary for candidates to have adequate skills in the use of computers and social networks.

As a result of these new tools, new jobs have arisen that were inconceivable a few years ago, such as Community Manager, responsible for virtual forums and communities, or the more technical ones in charge of promoting websites, such as SEO consultants. And S.E.M., which seek to achieve greater visibility in the networks of a given brand or company.

Young people have been incorporating the tools offered by this new technology into their lives, both academic and leisure, so that there are now many universities that partially or totally teach online, being able to connect from any fixed or mobile device, such as tablets, iPads, or smartphones.

The teachers have a double function: to organize and record the classes to be taught and to provide virtual tutoring to resolve any doubts that may have arisen from them.

This has enabled to open the doors of universities to students from all over the world, with the only requirement that they have the necessary language skills to follow the classes, and of course, a device with an Internet connection.

For this reason, the only thing that could not be resolved was when the exams were taken, which are required to be in person, either at the university itself or at a private school in the student's country. So that the student who takes the test has an adequate knowledge of the test's subject.

One way of guaranteeing the level of training achieved by the student, since otherwise, with the non-attendance exams, it is possible that someone else may answer it, without the student being the student.

In my particular case, after several years of teaching face-to-face in different universities, I had to take a training course in order to continue my teaching work, but this time through the Internet, for which I had to adapt the technological tools that I used to use to the new demands, including the familiarization of training platforms such as Moodle, or the employment of videoconferencing programs to teach online, which allowed me to give classes in Spain, both on the Peninsula and on the Islands, while they were followed from Latin America.

But there are risks of the Internet that emerge when youth leisure becomes almost exclusive in the intensive use of this technology, losing social contact and sometimes, with reality itself.

Many studies are being carried out in this respect, because of this new modality, where new cases of cyber addicts are detected every day, that is, people who are unable to disconnect from the network, facilitating social isolation, and the lack of mental and personal hygiene, also associated with inadequate food, but can we predict the future addiction to the Internet?

This is what we have tried to answer with a research carried out jointly by the Institute of Medicine, Kaohsiung Medical University and the Hsiao-Kang Municipal Hospital (Taiwan), the results of which have been published in the scientific journal J.A.M.A. Pediatrics.

Two thousand two hundred and ninety-three young people took part in the study and were followed for two years, being evaluated at 6, 12 and 24 months.

All of them were tested for addiction using the standardized C.I.A.S. scale. (Chen Internet Addiction Scale); levels of depression using the Chinese version of the C.E.S.D. scale (Center for Epidemiological Studies Depression); attention deficit hyperactivity disorder as assessed by the A.D.H.D.S. scale. (Attention-Deficit/Hyperactivity Disorder Self-rated Scale); social phobia using the F.N.E. scale. (Fear of Negative Evaluation); and the hostility of the participants through the B.D.H.I.C.-S.F. (Buss-Durkee Hostility Inventory-Chinese Version-Short Form).

The results report that those young men who had high levels of aggression showed higher levels of addiction after the age of 2, becoming the best predictor of this psychopathology.

In contrast, the adolescents who took part in the study showed that the best prognostic of future addiction is related to suffering from attention-deficit/hyperactivity disorder.

In both boys and girls, previous levels of social phobia and depression were not relevant for predicting future technology addiction.

The study also provides "revealing" information in that, in just two years, more than 10% of the participants were affected by Internet addiction and being insignificant the difference in the number of cases between male and female "addicts".

It is necessary to make studies in order to be able to create specific programs to prevent it, with special emphasis on education, as a decisive factor of self-regulation in the handling of new technologies, that is, with a correct education, it would be expected that the young will be able to use technology properly and not overuse it.

Although the phenomenon of Internet Addiction is recent, it has been evolving quickly, so the first addicts to video games or the Internet, spent hours and hours without leaving their rooms, unable to disconnect from role-playing games or any other video game to score more points and increase the ranking, as if that was the most important thing of all.

From these first cases, the term "hikikikomori" syndrome appeared, originally identified in Japan during the 1980s and 1990s.

Young people who suffered from it, turned their backs on society and refused to interact with others, except through computers, which sometimes resulted in poor nutrition and even the abandonment of personal hygiene.

An example of this has been observed to a greater or lesser extent all over the world, where the computer screen becomes the "reality" of the young, where nothing beyond the four walls of his room exists.

Nowadays, thanks to mobile devices such as tablets, iPads or Smartphones, you no longer need to stay at home to be connected to the Internet.

In addition, the emergence of social networks has increased the possibilities of communication, beyond video games or chat a few years ago, which has resulted in an increase in the number of cases of Internet addiction, but what is the percentage of addicts to Facebook?

This is precisely what the Department of Information System and the Department of Fundamentals of Education and Social Sciences, Faculty of Education, Malaysian University of Technology (Malaysia), together with the Department of Computer and Information Technology, Islamic Azad University (Iran), have tried to answer, the results of which have been published in the International Journal of Information and Education Technology.

The study included 441 university students, with an estimated average age of 24, of whom 49% were women.

All were tested using the standardized scale to determine the level of addiction to Facebook called B.F.A.S. (Bergen Facebook Addiction Scale); the level of control locus was also assessed using the L.O.C. (Locus of Control); and the one of personal selfishness through the Ego Strength Scale.

The results report that young people showed very high levels of addiction to Facebook, reaching 47% of them, which means that almost half of the Facebook users were addicted to this social network.

These data are maintained despite the origin (Malay or non-Malay), the religion they practised (Muslim, Christian, Buddhist...) and even the gender of the participants.

One of the limitations of the study is that the selection of the participants was made among those who habitually used social networks, that is, the results reflect that among the habitual users we can find these high levels of addiction, but it doesn't say anything about those young people who don't use social networks so often.

It should be considered that the study was only carried out with university students, and the results could not be extended to the rest of the population, or even to young people, since they may be influenced by such outstanding variables as the socioeconomic level or the culture of Facebook users, aspects that are not analyzed in this study.

Despite the fact that the authors of the study have chosen to analyze the levels of Facebook, due to the popularity of this network, and its growing number of users, which has now reached nearly two billion; there has been no comparative analysis with other social networks to try to understand if it is a phenomenon of Facebook, or any other network such as Twitter or Google+, so that new replicas are needed to establish this respect.

It will also have to be taken into account whether the addicts to Facebook are exclusively to this social network, or to all of them; if so, it would be more than a "problem" with Facebook, one of the personality of the individual that is reflected in their use of the Internet, but in order to know the answer to this question the design has to be improved, incorporating questions on the use of other social networks and their frequency of use.

Chapter 2. Symptomatology of Internet Addiction

Nowadays, it is difficult to find a student who does not regularly use the Internet for work or leisure, so he may be addicted to the Internet.

Every time new technologies are introduced at a younger age, almost from the first years of life, children now have tablets, and a few years later they have their own Smartphone, with Internet access.

Nowadays, even in schools, the use of new technologies is promoted through the use of tablets instead of books, in addition to the fact that the teacher uses his or her electronic blackboard, all of which is connected to the Internet, where specific reference materials are designed for the classes.

But when you start with the Internet, there is no limitation in its use, especially when you get into games or social networks, an activity that requires more and more time, until you don't know how to develop an addiction.

It should be taken into account that when we talk about addiction, we are not only talking about addiction to certain substances such as alcohol, tobacco or other drugs, since there is a category of addiction called behavioural.

Addictions are defined by their consequences in the daily life of the person suffering from it. Thus, an addiction is considered to be an addiction when the person involved in its planning or thought is excessive, interfering with its daily life; where there is a certain level of custom, needing each time new experiences or more quantity to maintain the desired effects; it can cause personal, social or work problems.

Behavioural addictions include the more commonly known as pathological gambling, and other less well known addictions such as work, sex, or Internet Addiction. Some characteristics of behavioural addictions include:

-Loss of control of the will.

-Spending too much time on that activity and taking it away from others, whether it is work or social relationships.

-Some level of isolation, unless they are "social addictions".

-With negative economic, emotional and family consequences due to this dependency.

-With "inclusions" of thoughts, making it difficult not to think about it, and causing an elevation of anxiety and uneasiness when a person lacks access to such an addiction for a while.

- With negative consequences on academic performance.

In some cases it also leads to a certain personal neglect that can be shown in a careless and unhygienic way.

What is going to be materialized in Internet Addiction through the following symptomatology:

-Psychomotor agitation when connected to the network.

-Anxiety when you have to do any other activity that is not on the Internet.

-Loss of control when you have to disconnect.

-Decreased decision skills, focused on staying as long as possible online.

-Academic grade reduction among students due to lack of attention in class.

-Motivational problems and cognitive regulation, because their thoughts are almost exclusively focused on their activities on the web.

-Feeling of isolation and loneliness, due to the incomprehension of others about their passion for new technologies.

-With a feeling that the world, outside the net, is boring, looking to spend their time watching "interesting" videos or conversations.

-Emergence of emotional problems, especially depression, caused by social isolation.

-Excessive spending of hours on mobile devices or computers connected to the Internet.

-Irritation when someone talks to you while you are online or tries to disconnect you from the network.

-Decreased face-to-face social interactions, preferring to do it through social networks.

All of this is explained by the same neural mechanisms that allow us to tend to repeat behaviours. The positive and enjoyable consequences of this are a great way to make learning easier.

Thus, the use of new technologies when they cease to be useful for work or everyday life and become "necessary" or "essential" may be leading to a technological addiction, whether it is the "excessive" use of new terminals, smartphones or tablets, or the intensive and "uncontrolled" use of instant messaging services such as Messenger, Whatsapp, Twitter or Tuenti.

This has led to the appearance of new phenomena that did not exist before, so new terms had to be created to contemplate it, as is the case of the F.O.M.O. (Fear Of Missing Out), or fear of missing out on the latest, that is, the need to be on the lookout for social networks at all times so as not to miss the last mobile device that came out or the last video of your favourite singer, first identified by the University of Essex (England) together with the University of California and the University of Rochester (USA) as reported in the scientific journal Computer in Human Behaviour.

This term is close to a new type of phobia related to technology called nomophobia, which refers to the fear generated by being disconnected from social networks or the Internet in general, caused by the impossibility of accessing a mobile device or computer; feelings that are also generated when the Smartphone is left without a battery or the wifi signal is "lost".

In order to study this in greater detail, research has been carried out at the University of California (USA) and the results have been published in the scientific journal U.C. Merced Undergraduate Research Journal.

In this study a bibliographic analysis was carried

out, for which the publications in PsycINFO and Google Scholar were analysed, taking into account that the term Nomophobia is so recently created that it is not yet included as an addiction by the D.S.M.-V (Diagnostic and Statistical Manual of Mental Disorders, currently in its fifth version).

This phobia has been seen first among young people, although it is not exclusive to them. Midway between obsession and addiction, nomophobia causes high levels of anxiety among those who suffer from it.

We must distinguish between this type of phobia, which mainly affects the cognitive level by increasing the levels of anxiety generated by "catastrophic" thoughts associated with not being able to connect, and Internet Addiction, which is a behavioural addiction, characterized by an incursion of thoughts that generate anxiety, followed by an addictive behaviour, which will cause the release of such anxiety, while providing satisfaction by connecting, and begins the cycle of addiction again.

Despite this distinction between Internet Addiction and nomophobia, these can occur in patients at the same time; although it is not exclusive, since it has been observed that Internet Addiction can also occur with obsessive-compulsive disorders, eating disorders or depression, among others.

One of the most accepted explanations regarding the origin and maintenance of this phobia is the theory based on the O.F.O.M. explained above, so that in many cases both terms Nomophobia or F.O.M.O.

are used interchangeably.

Another explanation, although more in the direction of Internet Addictions refers to the social reinforcement that comes with being continuously connected, as you receive "news" from other users, as well as their comments and updates.

Despite the above, and the fact that many cases have already been reported, there is still no prevention or intervention programme.

As with other behavioural addictions, such as shopping addiction, this phobia is socially accepted and not considered a problem.

In fact, health professionals are faced with the same dilemma as those faced with "legal" drugs, whether tobacco or alcohol, where the negative effects on health are known in the short and long term, but almost nothing can be done about prevention because it is legal.

The University of Villanova (USA), for the first time, has described a new phenomenon called "Sleep Texting", which refers to the fact of not having a regular sleep, as there are constant interruptions to read the messages received and send new messages. This phenomenon shows a decrease in the quantity and quality of sleep among young people, who are the main users suffering from it.

In this sense, research has been carried out jointly by the University of Washington and Lee University (USA) and the results have been published in the scientific journal Psychology of Popular Media Culture.

Eighty-three students participated in this study, which analyzed sleep quality levels using the Pittsburgh Sleep Quality Index, which provides information on three indicators: exhaustion, sleep problems and social relationships, with the aim of analyzing the influence of M.S.N. use. (text messaging) on the health of college students.

The results show how the three indicators were negatively affected as the number of messages they had to "manage" increased, but where the greatest effects were found were with regard to sleep problems, where from "moderate" levels of messages they already started to cause high levels of anxiety and with it difficulties to fall asleep.

The lower quantity and quality of sleep will have consequences for "daytime living", with less capacity for retention and attention among students, and if this situation continues over time, it can even affect health.

This is why it is important to "educate" the youngest in the use of these electronic devices, since, as has been indicated, they can generate problems of performance and concentration, as well as affecting their health and social relations and, most seriously of all, their health, due to the maintenance of high levels of stress and the lack of quality sleep.

And all this on the assumption that the person is "master of his will", that is, that he has not yet fallen into a technological addiction, which would have even greater negative effects.

The main problem with the detection of this type

of situation is that parents do not know how to assess the extent to which it is "normal" or has already crossed the line of what is appropriate and has become insane.

Likewise, the person who suffers from it, in spite of realizing the difficulties and harmful consequences that it brings him, is unable to recognize that he has a problem and that requires help from others to quit, even though he may need a specialist to overcome his addiction.

As can be seen from the previous result, the technology can cause serious difficulties in the person's daily life, to the extent that it can put his or her health at risk, as well as in the case of impairing the quality and quantity of sleep in order to have to answer the m.s.n. that are received.

As has been mentioned, one of the new realities of the developed society is that day by day technology has been occupying a prominent place in life.

So, from the moment someone gets up until they go to bed, all kinds of electronic devices are being used to make life more comfortable, but the technology is not just in the devices, but in what can be done with them, that is why a multitude of software (programs) have emerged to make the most of them.

Social networks have contributed to the interconnection of people, regardless of distance, offering immediate communication between friends and strangers, but the influence of these technological advances has certain risks for some people regarding mental health. Thus, clinics have even been created to deal with the addiction to technologies, due to the excessive use and abuse of them, which leads users to become addicted to them, but who is more sensitive to the addiction to social networks?

This is precisely what we have tried to answer with research conducted jointly by Kawasaki University of Medicine, Meiji University of Integrative Medicine and the Manaboshi Clinic (Japan), the results of which have been published in the scientific journal Psychology.

The study included 284 university students aged 18 to 24, of whom 144 were women.

They were all given a standardized questionnaire for the evaluation of addictions called S.N.Ss Addiction, and the level of loneliness perceived by the U.C.L.A. was also evaluated. Loneliness Scale, and self-esteem through the Interpersonal Trust Scale.

The data show that there are differences in the outcome of the level of addiction to social networks between men and women, with the former showing the highest number of cases of addiction.

The levels of addiction were not significant, depending on the degree of perceived loneliness or self-esteem of the participants.

One of the unexpected data pointed out by the authors was that they did not find any relation between the levels of loneliness or self-esteem and the addiction to social networks, as one might think.

Therefore, the addicted users to social networks do not seem to be isolated people, locked up in their homes, not even among those who exhibited low levels of self-esteem.

With regard to the selection of participants focused exclusively on university students, which limits the possibility of extrapolating the results to other populations, it is also necessary to take into account the characteristics of Japanese society, which is not present elsewhere, and new research is needed to analyze whether the results are maintained or not.

It should be remembered that the study does not separate the different social networks that are used, essential information, if you want to know the real impact of each of them on mental health.

Likewise, the age of the participants in the study excludes the most sensitive and even the most internet-sensitive people, teenagers, who are exposed to this addiction from an early age, so if some type of preventive intervention is planned; it is at this age that it is likely to be most effective.

Despite the previous, the study makes it clear that men are the most sensitive to this type of addiction, an aspect that has been explained by the authors, by the practical sense given by women, which "protects" them from becoming an end in themselves.

Some gender differences that raise the need to continue studying in order to understand why adults with the same level of education show a different disposition to addiction in something as new as the use of social networks.

But although there have been comments about the symptoms associated with Internet Addiction, it remains to be determined whether there is any relationship between this addiction and some kind of psychopathology, such as emotional addiction, for example, is there any emotional disturbance in Internet Addiction?

This is exactly what has been sought from research conducted by the Department of Zoology, University of Jahangirnagar; Mirpur Adhunik Hospital and Diagnostic Centre Ltd, University of the South; General Hospital, University of Health Sciences of Bangladesh; IBN SINA Hospital, Savar University; and Department of Public Health, Bangabandhu Sheikh Mujib University of Medicine (Bangladesh), the results of which have been published in the scientific journal Ec Psychology and Psychiatry.

The study included 400 university students, 44% of whom were women.

Two surveys were given to them, the first to evaluate the level of internet dependence through the Internet Addiction D.Q. and the second to check for the presence or absence of depressive symptoms through the CE.S.-D. scale (Center for Epidemiologic Studies Depression Scale).

The results show that 74.8% of the participants had depressive symptoms and 25.3% suffered from internet addiction.

A comparative analysis between the presence of depressive symptoms among students with and without internet addiction shows significant differences between them, being three times more likely to suffer from depression if they are internet addicted.

Among the limitations of the study is the fact that an evaluation was carried out using a questionnaire rather than taking other more objective measures to corroborate the data.

The authors do not put forward any explanatory theories on the relationship between depression and addiction, since they simply present the related data, without establishing which came first, that is to say, whether the addiction to the Internet has caused a feeling of isolation and depression; or whether suffering from depression has made the person more withdrawn in his or her social relationships and to take refuge on the Internet.

Finally, the study does not analyze the "content" of internet addiction, since it is not the same that it is addicted to social networks, where there is fluid communication with other users, as well as to video games, as this information could allow a better understanding of the different user profiles on the internet, and which of them are more at risk with respect to both addiction and depression.

In spite of the above, it is important to highlight two facts: firstly, that there is a serious health problem among the students evaluated in this country, since almost 75% of them show depressive symptoms; secondly, that they are three times more likely to suffer from depression if they are addicted to the Internet.

To complete these results, it would be necessary to establish an intervention plan, for which it would be necessary to study whether it would be more effective to do so on the Internet addiction, to see whether or not it reduces the depressive symptoms; or on the contrary, to intervene in the depressive symptoms to see if it reduces the Internet addiction.

Chapter 3. Diagnosis of Internet Addiction

The negative consequences of Internet Addiction on both academic performance and the socialization of young people with their peers have been discussed above, and in some cases it also involves some personal neglect that can be shown with dislike and lack of hygiene.

All of this is considered the expression of a behavioural addiction, which must be overcome with the intervention of a specialist, and which in many cases requires, as a first step, cutting off the child's access to the Internet, as would be done with other types of addictions, but is it possible to detect Internet addiction in young people?

This is precisely what we have tried to answer with research carried out at Payame Noor University (Iran), the results of which have been published in the International Journal of Behavioural Research & Psychology.

Three hundred and eighty high school students participated, of whom one hundred and ninety-four were women.

There were three main areas of study: first, to determine the extent to which young students are addicted to the Internet; second, to check whether the presence of addiction is related to the level of sincerity expressed within the family; and finally, if there are differences between the sexes in the previous two.

The standardized I.A.T. questionnaire was used for this purpose. to assess the level of Internet addiction of young people, and one created for this purpose to evaluate the level of sincerity at home of the participants.

The results report that boys experience significantly higher levels of addiction; similarly, the lack of sincerity within the family increases as dependency on the Internet grows, and therefore it is expressed significantly more in boys.

So it is possible to detect addiction among children simply by observing the level of sincerity of these in the family, when you start to look for excuses or to invent reasons to stay connected either through the computer or a mobile device, can be a good indication to suspect that the young person may be starting to suffer from Internet addiction.

This is a rule that cannot be applied to girls, since, despite suffering lower levels of Internet addiction, when they do so, they do not express themselves with less sincerity within the family, which in turn makes it more difficult to detect them and, therefore, to intervene to overcome them.

This would indicate that children are more sensitive to suffering from this type of addiction related to new technologies, which will have a negative impact on the quality of family life, trying to "hide" their addiction.

All of this can be used to establish prevention programs among the students themselves, to develop tools with which to deal with Internet addiction, and even among parents, so that they are clear about the first symptoms of addiction and can intervene as soon as possible.

Although the results are clear, more research is needed to reach conclusions in this regard, as it is a study focused on a population with specific characteristics, not being the country under study, Iran, among the top ten in terms of the number of Internet users, used daily by a little more than half of the current population (53.3%), is well behind countries such as Norway, Iceland, the Netherlands, Sweden and Denmark, all of them above 90%, according to data collected by Internetworldstats.

A concrete case of technological addiction is the addiction to video games, which emerged as a behavioural addiction long before Internet Addiction, becoming popular in the 80s, but the emergence of the Internet has done nothing more than facilitate and encourage this type of addiction, to which a player can devote more than eight hours a day.

Therefore, it would be a new form of gambling addiction, which is defined as a behavioural addiction in which the person loses control of his economy, modifying his scale of values, which can even lead to economic ruin, previously including the loss of friends, partners and even children.

From public and private institutions, foundations

and associations have tried to prevent as far as possible gambling, either by establishing minimum ages for access to the game, as creating a file of gamblers which you are banned from access to casinos, to avoid relapse.

On the Internet, however, these limits are not so clear, as one can "lie" and start gambling online at the age of 18.

Likewise, access is not limited to any user, no matter how many times they have lost in this type of game, whether in online casinos, internet poker games or any other type of game.

For people outside gambling, it may be thought of as a "minor" problem, but it should be remembered that it is a behavioural addiction, i.e. the person is going to spend a good part of their time trying to play, with intrusive thoughts about "what would have happened if they had gone out...", or "in the next game I will certainly recover".

And that's despite the fact that when they go to a gambling association they are told in detail that gambling machines and games of chance are designed to lose, that's precisely the business of casinos and slot machine owners. Even though the person knows that he or she will never be able to "beat" that probabilistic system mathematically created to make him lose, he still thinks and feels that "with a little more luck..."

Nowadays, the possibilities of online gaming are almost endless, from "classics" to multiplayer games and all kinds of games; you can even download them onto your smartphone and play at any time.

Although the tops of the most downloaded Apps (programs designed for tablets and smartphones) change from month to month, they all have something in common, they are usually free games, at least in the early stages, and as the person is added, the game is giving new possibilities in which to invest money, buying extras such as "powers", "time" or new phases.

Everything has been designed and thought out to get hundreds of thousands of dollars a year from players who get " addicted " to video games, but if among all these video games there is one that is particularly difficult to deal with, it is the one that corresponds to the addiction to " traditional " gaming, that is, where the first and last objective is money.

Previously in every bar in every city there was a "slot machine" with colourful sounds and images, nowadays its use is becoming more and more restricted, but there are still casinos where you can "look for luck" by gambling.

There are many people who have been ruined playing roulette, cards or any other gambling game, in fact, when I was in Las Vegas (USA) staying in one of the themed hotels in the city, what became clear to me is that it was only and exclusively a business.

The "slot machines" were priced annually and the amount of money they were capable of earning was estimated, if for any reason they lowered that rate by one of them, it was withdrawn and replaced by a more modern one that could "produce" more money.

Money that, of course, came out of the tourists who came to the city to "try their luck", with the dream or desire to turn their lives around with some of those mega prizes, which in some casinos could be up to a million dollars.

However, technology has introduced into the house this possibility of addiction to gambling with money, in the so-called virtual casinos, and to facilitate "the down payment", they give you money to bet the first time, to "try the honeys of success" and that makes you think that you can achieve more next time.

In this regard I share an interview with D. Cam Adair, co-author of the Manual on Addiction of Video Games for Parents, who reveals the keys to the effects and treatment of video games addiction.

How is video game addiction defined?

Addiction is a word used these days, often misused as an adjective for a type of obsession.

In my experience, I dropped out of high school and stopped working in order to play more. But, I think it's easy for us to get caught up in trying to define "video game addiction" instead of focusing on what's really going on with the players and why they're so attracted to the games themselves.

- Are there really more video game addictions than in the last decade?

Of course, of course! The ease of access (iPhones, iPads, etc.) to games has created opportunities for many more players to play than ever before. Statistics show that 100% of boys and 96% of girls between the ages of 8 and 18 use video games. The potential scale of this problem is much larger than we have considered in previous years.

- What are the symptoms of video game addiction?

I use the term W.A.S.P. to easily identify certain symptoms of video game addiction.

Withdrawals, Apathy, Social Relationships, Performance (W.A.S.P)

Anxiety - They experience mood swings or withdrawal symptoms when not gambling.

Apathy - Experiencing apathy toward other activities and/or their own health and personal hygiene.

Social relationships - Most of your relationships are online.

Performance - Your school or job performance grades are negatively affected.

These are just some of the ways to identify whether gambling is a bigger problem for a specific person. Many times, these types of symptoms develop over time as use continues.

- How do you suggest overcoming the addiction to video games?

My goal has always been to identify the cause of the problem and provide support to solve it. In my research I have found four main reasons why players play: that they provide a temporary escape, a social community, a sense of purpose and measurable steady growth.

The key to overcoming the problem is to find new activities that meet these same areas, while also working to improve their social skills. I suggest group activities like martial arts or joining a gym, where it is easier to make friends as positive steps forward.

What are the consequences of video game addiction?

The consequences are in relation to each person, but in general it seems to me that relationships are where the greatest consequences occur, and in the end, when it comes to video games, there is a difference between having fun and being happy. In my research I have found that many players who play for fun, but fullness and lasting happiness is not so common. It's about turning your life into the definitive video game.

Is video game addiction a problem in developed countries?

Actually, it is. But with increasing access to smartphones worldwide, it becomes a potential global problem in the coming years.

- Are there any personality qualities associated with video game addiction?

The most at risk players are those who identify with

the sense of isolation and rejection, especially if they happen in school, although much has also been said about social anxiety and depression as predictors.

Nowadays it is unthinkable that certain jobs can be carried out without a computer, whether working online or offline, in many cases it is necessary to consult information and the Internet or write an email to customers.

But this access to the Internet is not always accompanied by higher performance at the workplace, because it is sometimes "used" for leisure.

Gathering and answering personal emails, chatting and commenting with people outside the workplace about trivial matters, reading an electronic newspaper or searching the Internet about the upcoming holidays are no longer "inappropriate" behaviour in many workplaces, but are becoming habitual.

But Internet access is not limited to working hours, as it is also accessible and present when you leave work, and can affect and replace leisure time, but what is the profile of Internet addiction?

This is what we have tried to answer with a research carried out by the Department of Recreation, Faculty of Physical Education and Sports, University of Gazi (Turkey) whose results have been published in the scientific journal Universal Journal of Educational Research.

The study included 4,507 research assistants, aged

23 to 47, of whom 60.2% were women.

All of them were given an online questionnaire to assess the level of Internet addiction through the B.A.P.I.N.T. (Batery of Addiction Profile Index Internet Form), sociodemographic data were also collected from the participants, as well as questions relating to their leisure habits.

There were significant differences in gender, marital status, educational level, duration and perception of leisure time.

Where men get higher scores for Internet addiction; most of it occurring in singles. With regard to the level of education, the higher the level of addiction, the lower the level of addiction.

As for leisure time, it is inversely related to Internet addiction, that is, spending more leisure time, either with friends or going to the movies, prevents Internet addiction; although this leisure time must be of quality, because if you live as unsatisfactory the risk of Internet addiction increases.

One of the limitations of the study is with respect to the population analysed, the Turkish population, with very defined cultural characteristics, which makes it necessary to check whether these results are maintained in other populations.

Similarly, the evaluation of Internet addiction has not been accompanied by an objective measure, such as the time actually connected or what it does when it is connected.

The high number of participants in the study

makes it possible to establish a profile of Internet addicts according to the results, men, single, with low levels of education, who spend little time on leisure, and this is not satisfactory for them.

It is now necessary to establish prevention plans for this group of people who are more vulnerable to Internet addiction, an intervention that can be aimed at increasing the number of hours dedicated to leisure activities, ensuring that this time is satisfactory for the user.

At present, new indicators are being sought in order to establish a better diagnosis and even implement prevention programmes, but are there factors of individuals involved in Internet Addiction?

This is what has been tried to be answered with a research carried out from the Faculty of Psychology, Shandong Normal University (China) whose results have been published in the scientific journal Psychology Research.

Three hundred and sixty-three students between the ages of 17 and 24, half of whom were women, took part in the course.

All of them were given several standardized questionnaires to evaluate their level of Internet Addiction through the C.I.A.S.-R. (Chinese Internet Addiction Scales review), to learn about the level of stress experienced through the A.S.L.E.C. (Adolescent Self-Rating Life Events Check List); for the level of social support perceived through the P.S.S.S.S. (Social Support Scale) and to assess the level of aggressiveness, A.Q.

was used. (Aggression Questionnaire).

The results indicate that internet addiction is positively and significantly related to higher levels of aggressiveness and stress, and negatively to levels of social support.

That is, the higher the level of social support, the lower the aggressiveness, the lower the stress levels and the internet addiction, and the higher the internet addiction, the stress and anxiety levels, which leads to greater physical and verbal aggressiveness.

Among the limitations of the study is that it does not include measures of an observational or behavioural recording nature, as it is based only on the response of the participants.

It would also have been appropriate to take some measure of personality, to assess whether this media in internet addiction or aggressiveness.

By finding an intermediary role in the perceived levels of stress, between internet dependence and aggressiveness, it is possible to establish prevention and intervention plans to prevent this addiction from ending in aggressiveness.

Finally, but not least, the role of social relationships in the "real world" and especially in the family is fundamental to preventing both internet addiction and later aggressiveness.

There are still many questions parents and teachers have about how to prevent and detect Internet Addiction.

In order to respond to this problem, which is

becoming more and more frequent nowadays at T.E.A. Ediciones has published the ADITEC (Evaluation and Prevention of Internet, Mobile and Video Game Addiction) which is divided into two blocks, the first on detection and the second on intervention.

With respect to the first part, on the detection of Internet Addiction, three standardized questionnaires have been created, aimed at children between the ages of 12 and 17, with an estimated application time of 5 to 10 minutes each.

- ADITEC-I questionnaire for the detection of Internet addiction, where abuse is evaluated; abstinence; disturbance and absence of control and escape.

- ADITEC-M questionnaire for the detection of addiction to mobile phones, cell phones or smartphones, where tolerance and abstinence are evaluated; the difficulty to control the impulse; the problems derived from economic spending and abuse.

- ADITEC-V questionnaire for the detection of addiction to video games, where compulsive gambling is evaluated; abstinence; tolerance and interference with other activities; associated problems and escape.

For each of these dimensions, the questionnaire provides a score, which is compared with the scale according to gender, i.e. there is a scale for comparison with the general population of minors between 12 and 17 years of age for males, and another scale for females.

A total evaluation of the previous dimensions is

also obtained.

Obtaining a score translated into percentiles, where values close to 50 are considered "normal"; above 85 it is possible to think that the young person is at risk; while if it is higher than 95 it is possible to diagnose a Internet Addiction problem.

With regard to the second part, a cyber-addiction prevention programme has been designed for children aged 10 to 16 for each type of previous addiction, with three sessions of 50 minutes each.

Among the objectives of these programs is to inform about technological addictions, to sensitize minors about the negative consequences of their abuse, and to develop the necessary skills for their prevention.

The intervention is designed for collective application in the school setting, including presentations, videos of testimonies, illustrative cartoons, activities scheduled for individual work at home, and an initial and final questionnaire to evaluate the effectiveness of the programme.

An essential tool in clinical practice with adolescents, who are most exposed to the effects of the use and abuse of technology, and who must be more involved in establishing prevention policies aimed at education on how to make the most of technology without running the risk of being "hooked" on it".

In spite of the great progress made in having standardized tools for the evaluation of these addictions, not all the cases of Internet Addiction have been considered, leaving unevaluated Internet Addiction to gambling or sex, among others.

Likewise, the instrument has a fairly narrow range in terms of age of detection (12 to 17 years old) and prevention (10 to 16 years old), especially when it has been observed that Internet Addiction is "getting stronger" over the years and in the university stages it can affect more than half of the regular Internet users.

Chapter 4. Types de Internet Addiction

Some of the most frequent types of Internet Addiction, such as addiction to video games or social networks, have already been exposed, but in recent years the practice of sexting has become popular among young people, which is defined as the sharing of sexual texts, photos or videos through the Internet, a practice that is linked to the increase in the number of hours that young people spend in front of computers.

This has not been seen as a problem so far, since the importance is unknown, where some studies point to between 3 to 32% according to age, and whose effects are unknown how it affects young people but how does sexting affect minors?

This is precisely what we have tried to find out from research carried out by the Autonomous University of Madrid (Spain) and the National University of Entre Ríos (Argentina), the results of which have been published in the scientific journal Psicothema.

The study included 3,223 adolescents between the ages of 12 and 17, of whom 49.9% were women.

Among the characteristics of this population is that they spend an average of 2.21 hours per day and 3.02 on weekends spent on leisure on the Internet, i.e. excluding the time spent on school activities.

With regard to social networks, the most used is Instagram (64.8%), followed by YouTube (61.5%), WhatsApp (33.8%), Snapchat (18.3%), Twitter (13.6%), with Facebook (11.9%) being the least used.

All of them were administered the standardized questionnaire to detect sexting behaviours during the previous year called Sexting Questionnaire, to evaluate different personality characteristics the B.F.I.-S (Big Five Inventory) was used together with the G.SO.E.P. (German Socio-Economic Panel).

The results show that 13.5% of young people have practiced sexting in the last year, with 10.8% of those who have sent a message, 7.1% of those who have shared photos and 2.1% of those who have shared webcams with sexual content.

There were only significant gender differences in the sending of texts with a sexual content, with men (12.1%) being more likely to send them than women (9.4%).

There is a considerable increase in sexting practices as the age of minors increases, from 3.4% of sexting at 12 years of age to 36.1% at 17 years of age.

Regarding the personality characteristics present in the practice of sexting, there is a strong positive correlation with neuroticism and a negative correlation with extraversion.

That is to say, those young people with high levels of neuroticisms were the ones with the most sexting practices, and those with high levels of extraversion were the ones who shared the least sexting.

It must be taken into account that the results are obtained from the statements of the children, and not from the registration of their accounts to extract information directly, thus corroborating the extent to which sexting occurs or not, due to the problem of social desirability, for which the participant manipulates the response by answering according to what he or she believes is socially expected, for example, not recognizing the exact number of sexting practices.

Despite the above, it should be noted that the data are worrying to say the least, since one in three young people between 17 and 18 years of age frequently use sexting, which shows a lack of personal development.

Therefore, it would be a good idea to establish training plans for young people so that they can learn to relate to others in an appropriate way, especially to the opposite sex.

Chapter 5. Treatment of Internet Addiction

How many hours are "enough" in front of the computer, would be a question that all parents should ask themselves, when they see that children spend hours and hours on the screen of their computers.

The problem with Internet Addiction among the youngest is that they "make up" by consulting to do their homework, talking to friends or simply "resting".

There are several approaches to this problem, which try to give an account of the reasons for Internet Addiction.

From those who consider that this is a passing thing, which is "overcome" over time. Even those who see it as "normal" for a generation that was born with the technology.

From the psychopathological point of view, it cannot be understood as "normal" to a behavioural addiction such as Internet Addiction, so it is a question of looking for other alternative explanations which are dealt with by CyberPsychology.

One of the currently accepted explanations is that Internet Addiction or technological addiction is a way to "escape" or evade a reality that is sometimes traumatic for the person or not stimulating enough, but can Internet Addiction based on a previous trauma be explained?

This is what has been addressed by research conducted by Al-Farabi Kazakh National University (Kazakhstan) in conjunction with bChinese University of Hong Kong (China), the results of which have been published in the International Journal of Environmental & Science Education.

One hundred and eighty adolescents participated in the study, who were interviewed to learn their level of technology addiction.

The results show that only 7% of respondents were not cyber-addicted.

The 27% are at risk of Internet Addiction and the remaining 66% suffer from Internet Addiction.

To evaluate the level of trauma suffered by the student, the standardized scale called IES-R - Impact of Event Scale was used, sensitive to detect post-traumatic stress disorders.

The results indicate greater avoidance behaviour and higher levels of physiological activation, both characteristics of having suffered a trauma, among cyber-addicts versus non-technological addicts.

It should be pointed out that the study results are based on responses to standardized questionnaires and not on an actual observation of the child's behaviour.

Likewise, no information is provided on the gender of the participants, so it is difficult to know to what extent this significant relationship between trauma and Internet Addiction affects boys and girls equally or not.

Finally, as the authors indicate, there is a percentage of 27% who are at risk of suffering from

Internet Addiction, so it would be important to create mechanisms to detect this group in time to implement prevention policies aimed at strengthening social relations "away" from technology.

Likewise, for those young people who have suffered traumatic situations during childhood, schools and institutes should have qualified personnel to guide them and even refer them to specialized professional help when necessary.

Thus, we must try to break or at least weaken this relationship between the experience of trauma and Internet Addiction, using the latter as a mechanism to escape from an unpleasant reality.

But in order to establish these prevention mechanisms, the first thing to do is to realize the seriousness of the problem, which in the study represents more than half of the minors (66%), and how they are going to "drag" the consequences of a behavioural addiction such as cyber addiction throughout their lives.

As for the treatment, the first thing a person who suffers from a tendency to be almost obsessively connected to the Internet has to do is to recognize his or her dependence and the consequences it has on his or her life, as well as on those around him or her.

This step, which may seem simple, is one of the most difficult to achieve, as the person will seek any excuse not to take responsibility, minimizing the problem, justifying himself by saying that "he only checks the emails", or that "he does no harm by doing so".

As in other behavioural dependencies, the

treatment of Internet Addiction should include a combination of techniques that try to respond to the situation of anxiety and intrusive thoughts generated by the temptation to connect to the Internet, such as:

- Relaxation and breathing techniques, aimed at increasing the feeling of control over oneself in situations of temptation, as well as to control frustration when the person does not connect.

- Cognitive therapies, which seek the identification of those intrusive thoughts that aggravate the situation of tension that arises in front of an object such as a computer, a Smartphone or a Tablet that is a temptation to connect.

- Behaviour modification techniques that seek to reduce inappropriate behaviours by rewarding behaviours that do not involve the use of technology.

Conclusion

In this book we have tried to offer a broad vision of the problem of Internet Addiction, presenting current research conducted in different countries around the world, to present what is undoubtedly a global problem.

In some cases the figures are discouraging because of the number of young people who suffer mildly, moderately and even severely from this Internet Addiction, encouraged by the immediacy of communication and social networks.

This is why it is important to become aware of the problem, with the latest scientific data collected on this subject, and to establish possible ways of intervention that, without limiting the individual, do educate him/her so that he/she can make compatible his/her time "connected" to social life, which has become the best means of preventing Internet Addiction.

The first step is to prevent this problem from arising, but therapeutic strategies must also be developed for those already suffering from Internet Addiction.

About Juan Moisés de la Serna

He is a Doctor in Psychology, Master in Neurosciences and Behavioural Biology, and Clinical Hypnosis Specialist, recognized by the International Biographical Center (Cambridge - U.K.) as one of the 100 best health professionals in the world in 2010. He has taught at different national and international universities.

Scientific disseminator with participation in congresses, conferences and seminars; collaborator in various newspapers, digital media and radio programmes; author of the blog "Cátedra Abierta de Psicología y Neurociencias" and seventeen books on various topics.

He is currently working on research in the field of Big Data applied to Health, working with data from India, the USA and Canada, among others; this work is complemented by advice to technological startups oriented to Psychology and Personal Well-being.